G000076739

INTRODUCTION

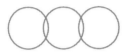

The mere fact that you've picked up this little book tells me something about you. It tells me that you already understand the value of forum. You know that forum is a place you can go to talk to other successful leaders about what's going on in your business and your life and get feedback in a trusting, confidential way.

Your picking up this book also tells me something else about you. It tells me that either:

- You and your peers are starting a forum, and you want to make certain you get a solid return for your investment of time and energy;

- You're already involved in a forum, and you want to ensure the experience continues to be a positive one and an efficient use of your time; or

- You're a member of a forum that is having some difficulties, and as a result, you're not realizing the benefits you had hoped for.

I feel fairly confident saying these things because I've been involved in forum for more than 25 years. I first learned about forum when I became a member of YPO (Young Presidents' Organization) as the CEO of a rapidly growing business. During my tenure at YPO, I participated in many forums as both a member and a facilitator. Because many of YPO's members are entrepreneurs, I learned a great deal about running forums. I also audited extensive facilitator training and, as a forum officer, was responsible for many of the YPO forums in North America at one point in my career. As a member of YPO's International Forum Board, I was part of a dedicated team of passionate individuals who spent 30 days each year solely on the subject of improving forums.

Through these experiences, I learned **the simple truth about forum: when it works, forum is life changing.** When it doesn't, forum can be a frustrating waste of time. (I also found that the need of CEOs and entrepreneurs for peer feedback is so great that sometimes a bad forum is better than no forum at all.)

So I set out to understand how forum works and, more importantly, why it works. I thoughtfully observed both successful and not-so-successful forums and analyzed their best practices as well as their mistakes. What I discovered is that while there is no clear-cut right or wrong way to conduct a forum, successful forums share common characteristics and cultures. Likewise, forums

THE PROCESS OF FOCUS FORUM™

WILLIAM MASTERS

www.FocusForum.net

THE PROCESS OF FOCUS FORUM

Copyright © 2013 William Masters. All rights reserved.

No part of this book may be reproduced in any form without written permission in advance from the publisher. International rights and foreign translations available only through negotiation with Perception, Inc.

Inquiries regarding permission for use of the material contained in this book should be addressed to:

Perception Inc.
150 Foothills Road
Greenville, SC 29617
Phone: 864-294-0490
Fax: 864-294-7563

Printed in the United States of America
ISBN: 978-0-9893271-0-7

Credits

Developmental & Contributing Editor:	Juli Baldwin, The Baldwin Group, Dallas, TX, Juli@BaldwinGrp.com
Copy editor:	Kathleen Green, The Baldwin Group
Design, art direction & production:	Melissa Cabana, Back Porch Creative, Plano, TX, Melissa@BackPorchCreative.com

CONTENTS

THIS BOOK BELONGS TO:

DATE:

FORUM NAME:

www.FocusForum.net

that get into trouble tend to make the same mistakes and experience similar problems.

Making a forum work is not as straightforward as it might seem. **The key to success is having a sound process. Following an established process keeps all members on the same page, operating under a set agenda and common guidelines.** A process also sets expectations for how members will interact and communicate with one another. Utilizing a forum process is the best way to hedge your bets and give your forum the greatest chance of success.

Based on everything I learned from studying and teaching various forum processes, as well as my experiences as a forum member and facilitator, I developed my own style and forum process, which I call **Focus Forum™.** My goal was to create a proven method that represents the best practices of forum. I've been using and teaching this forum process for more than a decade, achieving consistently exceptional results.

Focus Forum is different than other forum processes in several ways. First, it is designed to provide the highest possible value and benefit for members. While many forums advocate having 10 to 15 members, Focus Forum limits the number of members to between six and eight. I've found this to be the "sweet spot" for forum success, because every member gets enough "airtime," yet there are enough people to offer diverse opinions and input.

Second, **Focus Forums by design move very fast**, just as businesses must do in today's ever-changing marketplace. Focus Forum members get more done in the same amount of time as members in other types of forum. Third, Focus Forums are mostly self-run – they rely on the mutual commitment and responsibility of all members to make the forum work.

And finally, Focus Forum is designed primarily for entrepreneurs – the very people who usually need forum the most but often can least afford the time and cost unless the forum is effective and efficient. Many of the organizations that sponsor forums use moderators (with varying levels of skill and experience) to lead the forum. These moderators are often paid a handsome sum funded by the members. With Focus Forum, the cost of a forum is virtually nothing. You could say that Focus Forum is the forum process for the self-reliant person. In fact, Focus Forum can be used by just about anyone who wants to tap into the benefits of forum, including educational, church and non-profit leaders or even a group of leaders within a single organization.

This book outlines the simple yet powerful Focus Forum process that can be followed by any forum. The book is intended to be used as a guidebook – a how-to roadmap for building and maintaining an effective forum – and it will prove helpful whether your forum is running smoothly or plagued by problems. Specifically, it will cover:

- Members' roles and responsibilities within a forum;

- Ground rules for building mutual respect, commitment, trust, and above all, confidentiality;

- A detailed meeting agenda, including specific exercises and timeframes;

- Areas that forums should avoid in order to prevent potential problems.

It's not an exaggeration to say that forum changed my life and significantly enhanced my success. For this reason, I'm committed to helping others see forum as a unique opportunity to learn about life, understand how to run a successful forum, and avoid many of the challenges and pitfalls I encountered during my forum experiences. If my advice here can be of help in shaping successful forums and giving back to their members, then my work with forum will have come full circle.

Bill Masters

www.FocusForum.net

How to Get the Greatest Benefit from this Book

You want to give your forum the best chance for success. If your forum is successful, the odds are that its members, including you, will be more successful too (as will your business). To get the greatest benefit from this book – and the most out of your investment in forum – I recommend the following:

- Every member of the forum should have his or her own copy of this book and **read it at least once all the way through prior to the first meeting**. This ensures everyone understands the process, including roles, ground rules, agenda, exercises, etc.

- Members should bring their book to every forum meeting as a reference. **The Focus Forum Meeting Summary on page 64 serves as a recap of the process as well as an outline to follow during meetings.**

- Once the group selects a facilitator, he or she should carefully read the Focus Forum Facilitator

Guide, the third book in the Masters' Focus Forum™ Series. It covers the how-tos for effectively leading a forum.

● Take advantage of the forum tools and resources – many of them free – available at **www.FocusForum.net**.

Should your forum run into any problems not addressed in this book, the facilitator guide or the tools and resources available at **www.FocusForum.net**, feel free to contact me at wmasters@kinetixx.com.

CHAPTER ONE

THE ART AND SCIENCE OF FOCUS FORUM

A successful forum represents the confluence of art and science.™

The art of forum is the content – the issues, challenges and problems we bring to the group, as well as our feelings about those issues. Content is the "heart" of forum, the emotional element.

Most people think that forum revolves around business issues, but that is only partially true. Although business concerns may drive the initial content, typically, forum content eventually turns to personal challenges. These can range from death or illness of a parent, spouse or child, to financial problems and divorce, and everything in between.

Our business lives and our personal lives are intertwined, and that is why both contribute to the content of forum. Our business challenges often impact our personal lives, and our personal problems frequently have a negative effect on our businesses. The stress and worry caused by personal problems can weigh on us just as heavily (if not more so) as those caused by business challenges. Sometimes we just need to get things off our chest, and forum is a place we can do that. Not only is it allowed within forum, it's encouraged.

The science of forum is the process that we follow – the "rules" or guidelines regarding how we will interact with one another. **If content is the heart of forum, process is the "head" of forum, the logical element. The process of Focus Forum is broken down into three key areas:**

1. **Ground rules** for how we will treat each other;

2. The **roles and responsibilities** that are necessary in order for a forum to effectively operate; and

3. The **process, structure and format** of forum meetings.

I often refer to forum as being similar to the sandbox we played in as children and to the process of forum as the unwritten rules of the sandbox. Children who threw sand at other children or didn't play nicely weren't allowed back in the sandbox. If a bully showed up, everyone else left. The process of forum provides the rules by which we can all "play" together nicely inside of a forum. Having guidelines minimizes opportunities for misunderstanding, allows the content to come through and keeps us out of trouble as we get into the emotional aspects of a problem. Furthermore, the process helps to create a culture in which members with overbearing personalities are tempered and those who are quiet are encouraged. As a result, no one dominates the group, and everyone has the opportunity to participate.

I find that people often underestimate the importance of process to the success of a forum. Yet if we stop to think about it, we realize that processes and rules are crucial to how we function in many areas of our lives. We obey traffic laws, for example, which are simply the rules for how we will interact with one another on the road. When everyone follows the rules, the result is a safe, expedient environment. But consider what happens when people don't follow the rules of the road. Sadly, people die every day because someone runs a red light, doesn't yield or otherwise doesn't follow the rules.

Of course, following the rules of forum is not a life-and-death situation – at least not in terms of human life. But the truth is, when we don't follow the process, forums often die. **Forum is based on an evolving trust and a shared life together.** As in any relationship, any time we do something harmful to another member (even unintentionally), it takes time to heal that hurt, and sometimes the scars never completely go away.

If a member betrays another member's trust or breaches the confidentiality of the group, it is very difficult to salvage the forum and restore it to a place of trust. **Without trust and confidentiality, there will be no content because people won't be willing to open up and share.** And without content, there is no value to the forum. People will lose interest and quit coming. Once that happens, the forum is dead and should be disbanded. As the saying goes, "When riding a dead horse, dismount."

Although both content and process are crucial for a successful forum, process must come first. Process is the secret to making forum work. Consequently, the rest of the book will focus almost exclusively on process. When we stay within the process, we create a safe environment where we can be open and honest. As we disclose details about our businesses and our lives and others accept us in a nonjudgmental way, trust develops and content begins to naturally emerge. Once a forum experiences several high-level content issues, members start to genuinely bond and truly care about one another.

As the forum moves to the next stage, we become comfortable both giving and receiving constructive and sometimes difficult feedback. And after all, isn't that the main reason we join a forum to begin with? **Forum is the place we go to ask the questions we can't ask anyone or anywhere else. When life gets tough, forum is where we go to get candid input and frank advice.**

Forum is also a place where we can learn about ourselves. My forum experiences have given me deep insights into myself, made me a better person and allowed me to better understand people who are different than me. The personal development that occurs through forum is similar to the concept of the Johari Window.

The Johari Window model was developed by Joseph Luft and Harry Ingham in 1955. It is comprised of a square with four quadrants:

	KNOWN TO SELF	**NOT KNOWN TO SELF**
KNOWN TO OTHERS	**Public Self** I know, you know	**Blind Self** I don't know, you know
NOT KNOWN TO OTHERS	**Private Self** I know, you don't know	**Unknown Self** I don't know, you don't know

This diagram is based on the Ingham and Luft Johari Window[1] and a Johari window developed by Samuel Lopez de Victoria, Ph.D.,[2] and adapted by William Masters.

[1]Proceedings of the western training laboratory in group development (1955), Volume: 5, Issue: 1, Publisher: University of California, Pages: 4

[2]López De Victoria, S. (2008). The Johari Window. *Psych Central*. Retrieved on April 4, 2013, from http://psychcentral.com/blog/archives/2008/07/08/the-johari-window/

The Public Self represents what we know about ourselves that others also know about us, such as our behavior, skills and attitudes. The Blind Self represents things we do not recognize in ourselves but others see in us. For example, I might see myself as a funny guy, but others don't think I'm amusing. Or, I might not consider myself to be a good public speaker, yet others do.

The Private Self represents what we know about ourselves that others don't – perhaps our weaknesses or things that are embarrassing to us. And the Unknown Self represents those things that neither we nor others know about us. Once at a forum retreat, we played football on the beach, and I discovered that a fellow forum member was incredibly fast. Because I had never played sports, I didn't know people were that much faster than me, and the other forum members never knew I didn't know that, as most people have a basic understanding of sports.

When we disclose information about ourselves in forum, we enlarge our Public Self and shrink our Private Self. And with the help of feedback and insights from other members, we are able to minimize our Blind Self. Forum even helps us reduce our Unknown Self as we learn together as a group. For instance, another member may share a business challenge they are facing concerning product liability. During the course of the discussion, we come to realize that product liability could potentially be a problem for our business, something we had never considered before. In many respects, the Johari Window represents the essence of forum – enlarging our "knowns" and minimizing our "unknowns." **Forum is a place to make discoveries about ourselves and life through various experiences about and between each other.**

Perhaps my favorite analogy for forum is that it is like an orchestra. In an orchestra, each musician artfully plays his or her instrument, yet everyone must play their parts together to make a song. The orchestra is led by a conductor who keeps everyone on tempo and understands when to bring out and highlight each part. In forum, we play our part by bringing our problems as well as our insights and experiences. The process of forum is how we play our music together. The forum facilitator, like the conductor, keeps us on track and in sync, all playing the same song. The result is the beautiful music of life.

Forum can be truly life changing. **I believe, at its core, the very idea of forum is that we are there to share time and play our life's music together. As we come to understand the richness of this music, we become a better instrument and more harmonious with everyone we share our lives with.**

www.FocusForum.net

CHAPTER TWO

GROUND RULES FOR A SUCCESSFUL FOCUS FORUM

Although we usually are not consciously aware of it, we follow "rules" in our relationships that guide how we communicate, treat each other and develop trust. These guidelines are often unspoken, yet they exist in virtually every successful relationship, be it a marriage, a sports team, a team at work or a group of friends. For a forum to be successful, we need the same kinds of relationship rules. **Without a conscious and intentional process for fostering relationships among forum members, the chances of the group developing a connection and staying together diminish greatly.**

Just like some relationships, some forums never develop the "chemistry" necessary to sustain the group long term. If you find that to be the case with your group, I encourage you to leave and find another forum that is a better fit for you. However, unless there is a major conflict of interest, **I strongly recommend you stay with a forum for one year, because it takes time to**

build the relationships and culture that make a forum successful.

When we join a forum, we are in effect agreeing to become emotionally intimate with a group of people who may be complete strangers or acquaintances at best. **A forum is not the place for existing friends to come together, but rather a place to develop new friends.** Forum is all about putting yourself and your challenges "on the table" for everyone to see. This is why trust is paramount for any forum. If we do not trust one another unequivocally, then we won't be open to sharing the truth in our lives.

So how can we proactively and quickly develop relationships and build trust within a forum? **We must establish clear ground rules for how we will treat each other, work together, communicate and ensure confidentiality. We do this by agreeing on and committing to shared value norms and shared process norms.** Although each forum establishes its own norms, there are some basic norms that all forums should follow. Let's take a look at these.

SHARED VALUE NORMS

Our values represent our beliefs about what is acceptable behavior. Taken together, they form our code of conduct. A set of common shared values serves as a forum's "social etiquette" and ensures the group can work together in harmony. **While a forum may have many shared values, the most critical are confidentiality, mutual respect, mutual commitment and honesty.**

1. CONFIDENTIALITY

Confidentiality is key to building trust. When we open up and share details about ourselves and our businesses, we must be able to trust that other members will hold that information in the strictest confidence. Forum must be a safe place where we can reveal our most challenging problems, our most personal thoughts and our deepest fears.

In forum we have three types of confidentiality. **Forum Confidentiality means that issues are kept private within the group.** We never talk to anyone outside of the group about what goes on in the forum, but we can talk to other members (both during and outside of meetings). Let's assume, for example, that I share a business problem at a meeting. The following week, two other forum members meet for lunch. It is within Forum Confidentiality for them to discuss how they might help me with my problem, but they cannot discuss it with anyone else. **Everything said in a forum meeting is considered Forum Confidentiality by default unless it is specifically designated otherwise.**

With **Individual Confidentiality, forum members may not speak about an issue with anyone – including other forum members – unless the person who shared the issue expressly gives permission.** For instance, if a member confides to the group that they suspect their spouse is having an affair and indicates Individual Confidentiality, other forum members may not discuss that issue with each other. They can only discuss it with the member who presented it.

Absolute Confidentiality means no one may speak about the issue at any time with anyone, including the member who presented it. Occasionally, a member may share a topic that is so sensitive or emotional that he or she does not want it discussed again. An example might be a member who reveals he has prostate cancer and is so overwhelmed with feelings that he doesn't want to discuss the matter with anyone. Absolute Confidentiality is sometimes referred to as "nobody, nowhere, no time," meaning speak to nobody, nowhere, at no time under any circumstances.

Confidentiality breaches are a serious matter because they violate the group's trust. Yet they are often unintentional – it's all too easy to let something slip during a casual conversation.

Consider a scenario in which a member shares with the group that their business is experiencing financial difficulties. Later, at the forum holiday party with spouses, another member asks the member who disclosed the issue, "So how are your business numbers…have they improved any?" in the presence of the spouse. This is the first the spouse has heard of any financial problems and confronts the member about it. I've seen inadvertent confidentiality breaches like this countless times over the years.

Confidentiality breaches have a huge negative impact on both the individuals involved and the group as a whole. Nothing will shut down a forum more quickly than a confidentiality breach, so it is crucial that confidentiality is consistently observed. Your best bet is simply to remember, "nobody, nowhere, no time." (For details on how to handle a confidentiality breach, see Forum FAQs.)

2. MUTUAL RESPECT

Like confidentiality, mutual respect is one of the foundational legs of forum. It is, quite simply, the **Golden Rule: do unto others as you would have them do unto you.** Give your undivided attention to other members' presentations (no texting or checking email), just as you want them to pay attention during your presentation. Offer constructive feedback in a way that you would like others to give you constructive feedback. Be respectful of others' time like you want them to be respectful of yours.

Another way we can demonstrate mutual respect is by using what we call Forum Speak (technically known as Gestalt Language Protocol). Forum Speak means to speak from your personal experience rather than giving opinions or advice. Sharing personal experiences and their outcomes using "I" statements (such as, "When I found out that my father had Alzheimer's, this is how I felt and this is the process I went through...") is non-threatening and non-judgmental.

Forum Speak also allows various members to express differing points of view without getting into a debate as to who or what is right. It is also a very powerful way to help others see their blind spots – things we know about them that they do not know about themselves (remember the Blind Self in the Johari window?). Consider the difference between, "When I wore my hair long, I made fewer sales" versus, "If you want more business, you should cut your hair." The first is a valuable piece of business information; the second is an opinion and a judgment. Which do you think will be better received?

Telling someone they "should" have done this or "should" not do that is what we call "shoulding" on someone. As you might guess, shoulding on other people puts them on the defensive, causing them to either argue or shut down. And yet we frequently see this behavior in the early phases of a forum because executives and entrepreneurs are accustomed to expressing their opinions and giving orders. And because no one likes to be told what to do, shoulding diminishes rather than builds mutual respect.

For free resources on how to use Gestalt Language Protocol in forums, visit **www.FocusForum.net**.

3. Mutual Commitment
Highly successful people often see themselves as different or special and think that the rules don't apply to them. Now, put six to eight of these personalities in a room together. If there is not a steadfast commitment from everyone to follow the rules, we simply are not going to have productive meetings.

For forum to work, everyone must be "all in." Each and every member must fully commit to the forum as a whole. We must promise to attend every meeting, follow the process and actively participate. In addition, we must mutually commit to each other as individuals. We must pledge to confidentiality and respect…I won't text during your presentation, you don't text during mine. And above all, we must commit to give of ourselves fully – to be open and honest in sharing our lives with one another. One of my favorite quotes about mutual commitment is from Isabel Allende: **"We only have what we give."**

4. HONESTY

This might seem fairly straightforward, but **being honest – truly, gut-wrenchingly honest – is more difficult than one might think.** It's human nature to want others to accept us, to believe in us and to agree with us, and because of that, sometimes we might not be completely honest. We might sugarcoat our explanation of a situation or omit certain details to make ourselves look better to our peers. Or perhaps we manipulate our presentation so that others will see things our way, and we will get the "answer" that we want.

Being honest means being emotionally naked with the group – telling the whole truth about ourselves, the situation at hand and how we feel. Think about the Johari Window – honesty expands our Public Self and diminishes our Private Self, allowing us to grow and develop as people and as business leaders.

Honesty also involves being honest with yourself. One of the tremendous benefits of forum is that it makes us look in the mirror, so to speak, and see ourselves for who we are and where we are in our lives and in our businesses. **Oftentimes in forum we discover the truth about ourselves not through presenting and receiving feedback, but by observing someone else.** It's not easy to be honest with oneself – sometimes it's even a bit scary. But when we can see the truth of who we are, we can begin to change for the better.

One of the terms we use in forum is Clean Talk, which means telling the truth all the time – when you are giving presentations and when you are giving feedback. Don't embellish the story when you share an issue with the group. Remember, you are there to get advice, not to win a popularity contest.

Using Clean Talk is equally important when you're offering feedback. Let's face it – it can be difficult to tell others the truth, especially if it's something they don't see about themselves. It's often easier to just tell them what we think they want to hear. But that is not what forum is about. **The very essence and purpose of forum is to give and to get honest feedback as we share our life's experiences.**

SHARED PROCESS NORMS

Successful forums take their shared values and translate them into specific behaviors, which drive the forum process. These shared process norms are the rules we all agree to follow during meetings. Your group may agree to more, but the following four are the basic process norms that are critical to forum success:

1. ACTIVE PARTICIPATION

Active participation is an absolute requirement for forum. It has four fundamental characteristics:

● **Consistent attendance.** The key word here is "consistent." As you'll discover later in the book, a great deal of content is discussed at every meeting. When we skip a meeting, we fall behind with what is happening in everyone's life, and there is no way to fill people in on what they missed. Forums generally meet about 10 times a year, including a holiday gathering and a retreat, so consistent attendance is not an unreasonable commitment. If you miss a meeting, there should be a very good reason. If you miss two meetings, it had better be an exceptionally strong, life-altering reason. If you miss three meetings without a life-altering reason, you need to voluntarily remove yourself from the forum.

● **Being on time.** Almost by definition, entrepreneurs and executives are extremely busy; we're all in the same boat in that respect. Yet if we have agreed to respect one another, then we also must value each other's time by always being punctual. Consider the collective worth of a forum's time: If on average each member's time is worth $300 per hour and there are eight members, the collective value of the forum's time is $2,400 per hour. If just one member is 10 minutes late and the forum has to wait to start the meeting, that person just cost the forum $400. The truth is that a member's reason for being late is rarely more important than the group's time. Some forums charge members for being late, such as $10 per minute, to encourage punctuality.

● **Staying for the entire meeting.** A key aspect of the value of forum is learning from other members' experiences – not only in response to *your* presentation, but also in response to others' presentations. **Oftentimes we discover as much about ourselves by helping another member work through their challenges as we do working through our own.** Leaving meetings early shortchanges everyone, including you. It's like walking out of a restaurant having paid only part of your bill. You have received more

than you've given, because you have presented
and received feedback on your issue without
listening to and giving feedback on others' issues.
**Committing to a forum means arriving on
time and staying until the end.**

● **Attending the retreat(s).** Some forums have
one retreat per year; others have two – one more
focused on "work," the other more focused on
"play." Retreats typically last two to three days
and offer some of the most profound learning
and development opportunities. I often hear
forum members say they can't take that much
time away from their businesses, yet the forum
retreat is one of the most powerful ways they
can ensure their business's ongoing success.

2. **BEING FULLY PRESENT**
**Being fully present means we are completely
focused on and engaged with what is going on
in the meeting.** Our thoughts and emotions are
"inside the room." We are actively communicating,
jotting down questions to ask, giving feedback
and making notes to give other presenters. Being
fully present in a forum meeting is like being in
a soccer game. You can't stand on the field and
simply watch the ball go back and forth. You have
to be involved, focused on the game and giving it
everything that you have. If you are fully engaged
in a forum, giving and taking with all of your

energy, you will know it! By the end of the meeting, you will be tired yet invigorated.

One of the key ways to demonstrate being fully present is by not thinking about our business, checking email or texting. Every time you check email, take a telephone call or listen to a voicemail, your focus shifts away from the forum. As you deal with the distraction, you become even more focused on the outside issue, and it becomes very difficult to get your head back into the forum. These kinds of interruptions disrupt the harmony of the forum, much like a string breaking on a violin during a concert disrupts the music. Not to mention that these disruptions are disrespectful and discourteous to other forum members.

Being fully present in a forum meeting is so vital that most forums set a rule that members may not make phone calls, check email or voicemail or text, even during bio breaks. One way to minimize these disruptions is to charge a "connection fee," for example, $10 to $20 per phone call, email or text. (Any money collected helps pay for the retreat.) This is not about making money, but rather, forcing us to consider how important that call, email or text really is relative to the business of the forum.

Think of it this way. Would you check your email while you were at dinner with an important client? If you went to a concert, would you keep your telephone on? If you were in a meeting with your attorney or accountant, would you take a call from the office or check your voicemail? Hopefully, the answer is that you would not, especially if you are paying for their time. If you wouldn't disrupt these important meetings, the same should also be true of forum.

The bottom line is this: **If we are committed to the forum, we turn off our cell phones and email.** Of course, there are rare occasions when a member has a legitimate need to reconnect with the office or is expecting a truly critical phone call. If that is the case, the member states this at the beginning of the meeting and explains the nature of the situation. However, such critical situations are few and far between.

3. **ACTIVE LISTENING**
   Active listening is listening to understand the complete message being communicated. It is not only hearing the words the other person is saying, but also listening for what they are *not* saying. I often refer to active listening as "listening with forum ears," meaning that we pay attention to context, tone of voice, facial expressions, body

language and emotions. We must listen not only with our ears, but also with our eyes, our heads and our hearts. Active listening in a forum meeting is like playing with other skilled musicians. We become adept at identifying the nuances within the message or the song.

We demonstrate active listening by:

● Staying focused on the person speaking and not allowing our mind to wander. (If you start to lose focus, try taking notes or repeating back to yourself what the speaker said.)

● Using correct body posture, such as facing the person speaking, leaning slightly forward and maintaining eye contact when not taking notes.

● Asking questions during the clarifying phase of a presentation to demonstrate that we understood.

Active listening is a skill that we all should develop because it helps us communicate better with family members, employees and everyone else in our lives. Forum meetings give us the opportunity to practice and improve this skill, just as a musician practices a new piece of music until he or she can play it effortlessly.

4. BEING OPEN

When we are open, we allow ourselves to share deeply personal information, to show emotions, to be vulnerable and to take risks. Being open requires us to take the leap of faith that others in the group will accept us for who we are – the good, the bad and the ugly. We demonstrate openness when we make our presentations and share our problems with the group. But we also show our willingness to be open when we give feedback to others by sharing our personal experiences – both positive and negative.

Like so many aspects of forum, being open goes both ways. In addition to being open when we share our lives with others, we also must be open to receive. In this context, being open means accepting feedback in a non-defensive manner, being receptive to ideas that might be outside our comfort zone and being willing to accept help. I have found that simply saying "thank you" to feedback allows me to be less defensive and gives me time to absorb and consider the feedback.

Based on these foundational guidelines, each forum establishes its own distinct shared value and shared process norms. Once agreed upon, the norms are put in writing in a document that all forum members sign as an indication of their commitment to follow the norms. A sample Focus Forum Norms Constitution can be found in the "Forms and Resources" section at the back of this book.

Did you know there are unwritten "rules" for playing in an orchestra? Here are just a few:

- Check with your stand partner to make sure you can both comfortably see the music.

- The person on the left of the stand usually turns the pages of the music.

- Listen not just to your own part, but to everything else that is going on around you.

- Don't talk or whisper when the conductor is rehearsing other sections and you're not playing.

- Play with confidence and don't be afraid to make a mistake.

- Respect others by not practicing while others are tuning.

- Don't text or check your electronic device when the conductor is working with another section.

- A pleasant attitude makes for a player whom others want to have around.

Sound familiar? Similar to an orchestra, the ground rules of Focus Forum create the culture of the group. They set the stage for our interpersonal interactions, define what is acceptable behavior, prevent misunderstandings and help us make our music together.

CHAPTER THREE

THE ROLES OF FOCUS FORUM

Focus Forum utilizes a self-run approach, which means that responsibility for running the forum falls to the members themselves. In other forum processes, such as Vistage® and TAB (The Alternative Board)®, the forum is run by an outside moderator who charges a fee to moderate the forum and whose skill sets can vary widely.

I advocate self-run forums because I believe it has several advantages over other types of forum. Without a paid facilitator, self-run forums are more cost effective for members, which means virtually anyone can participate. Furthermore, based on my experiences, **members of self-run forums tend to be more loyal to the group because they have committed their time, energy and effort and therefore are more invested in seeing the forum succeed.** And finally, members get more value out of forum when they actively participate in running it.

Vistage is a registered trademark of Vistage International, Inc. The Alternative Board is a registered trademark of The Alternative Board.

In self-run forums, each member plays a role, and it's important to clearly define these roles so that every member understands how they fit in and what they are supposed to do. First and foremost, **each person must play the role of committed forum member.** As we discussed in the last chapter, that means making a commitment to the group as well as a commitment to follow the shared value norms and process norms.

In Focus Forum, however, there is an additional commitment above and beyond simply being a committed member. **When we join a Focus Forum, we are agreeing to accept the responsibilities of running the forum.** All members must take turns filling the various roles. Occasionally, there will be people who want to be in the forum yet won't want to help run it. But there is no room for freeloaders in a Focus Forum. Those who are not willing to do their part "need not apply."

Ideally, members volunteer for positions and are confirmed by a vote of all members. The criteria for any position are, first and foremost, does the person want to do the job, and secondly, do they have the capabilities to do the job. If someone has the desire but not yet the ability, the other members of the forum share the responsibility and help mentor that person along.

Forum roles are held for a limited time based on the norms of the forum, typically 18 to 24 months. You want to stay in a role long enough to master it, yet not so long that you get burned out. The role of facilitator, for instance, can be mentally taxing trying to stay on top of everything that goes on during a meeting. In addition, because the culture of the group tends to reflect the leader's personality, it's a good idea to periodically change things up.

Now that we understand their importance, let's take a look at each of the key roles:

THE FACILITATOR
Perhaps the most critical role in forum is that of the facilitator. Most other forum processes refer to the forum leader as the "moderator." Focus Forum utilizes a "facilitator." The difference between a moderator and facilitator is subtle yet crucial. A moderator *controls* while a facilitator *assists* and *guides* the forum. I have found that high-performance individuals subconsciously resist being controlled and are more open to being guided.

Going back to our orchestra analogy, the facilitator is similar to an orchestra's conductor. Just as the conductor leads musicians through rehearsals and performances, the facilitator leads forum members through meetings and retreats. A conductor sets the tempo, keeps the musicians in sync, communicates transitions between different sections of the music and corrects any mistakes the musicians might make. Likewise, a forum facilitator keeps the group moving forward together, makes certain they follow the process, maintains the tempo of the meeting by transitioning from one activity to another, and makes necessary adjustments if the group strays from the process. Just as musicians take their cues from the conductor, forum members take their cues from the facilitator as he or she guides them through the process.

The finest music conductors bring out the best in the musicians, shaping the music and turning it into something powerful and moving. The finest facilitators bring out the best in a forum's members, shaping our journey together into a life-changing experience.

The facilitator also makes certain that all members follow the ground rules for building trust and ensuring confidentiality so that forum interactions stay within the "safe zone." Effective facilitators have good active listening skills and are strong enough to lead a group of highly successful individuals. A facilitator must be willing and able to stop a presenter who rambles on too long, help members receive and accept honest feedback, redirect a member who starts should-ing on others, and keep peace and harmony within the group during difficult discussions. I often think of the facilitator as a shepherd who can both reassure members when they feel vulnerable and bring strong-willed members who wander off back into the flock.

Not everyone has the ability to be a good facilitator, and not everyone necessarily has to be the facilitator. However, I encourage all forum members to consider taking on the facilitator role, because **being a forum facilitator offers high-level leadership training that will pay big dividends in any situation that involves dealing with people.** To support facilitators in their crucial role, I created the Focus Forum Facilitator Guide, which shares extensive, detailed instructions on how to run a forum, including schedules, exercises, tips and techniques.

ASSISTANT FACILITATOR/ FACILITATOR-IN-TRAINING

In self-run forums, the facilitator is also an active member of the group. When the facilitator gives his or her updates or presents issues to the group, an assistant facilitator takes over to lead the group. **The assistant job is in essence a facilitator-in-training position that allows other forum members to learn and practice the key leadership role.** The assistant might be next in line for the facilitator position, or they could simply be a consistent support person.

PROCESS KEEPER

While the facilitator is responsible for leading the forum, the process keeper, as the name implies, is responsible for overseeing the forum process. Oftentimes, facilitators are so intensely focused on a presenter or so absorbed leading the forum that they don't notice when the process is slipping. **The role of the process keeper is to back up the facilitator in these instances and get the process back on track in order to keep the forum running smoothly.**

Think of the process keeper as the forum referee who sets the boundaries for what is done, how it's done and when it's done. He or she should be very familiar with the rules of forum and must be willing to speak up if they see a process being violated. If, for example, another member were to start asking questions during someone's presentation and the facilitator didn't stop it, the process keeper would step in and address it.

SCRIBE

The scribe's primary responsibility is to listen to what is being said during updates and then write that information on a flipchart in such a way that it can be recalled and understood by the presenter. (In the next chapter, I will describe exactly how the scribe records this information.) Although it's not necessary for the scribe to be a good speller, having legible handwriting is a must. Perhaps **the most critical skill for a scribe is active listening** – not only hearing what the presenter is saying, but also reading between the lines to understand the full message being communicated. For this reason, the scribe must be fully present and committed to the role. (In addition to the primary scribe, a secondary scribe should be appointed to take over when the primary scribe gives their presentation. In some forums, the process keeper fills the role of secondary scribe.)

TIMEKEEPER

As you will discover in the next chapter, time budgeting is a key aspect of the Focus Forum process. **Creating and sticking to a time budget ensures that every member gets their allocated, fair share of time to make presentations and get feedback. The timekeeper's role is to support the facilitator in making sure the group stays within the time budget.** The timekeeper acts as the forum's "metronome," keeping the members on tempo. For instance, during the initial updates (each no longer than eight minutes), the timekeeper would say, "Six minutes" at the six-minute mark to let the presenter know time is almost up. If the presenter was still talking at eight minutes, the timekeeper would simply say, "Time." These polite reminders give presenters the opportunity to wrap up their comments and reign in those presenters who tend to ramble and run long.

Over the years, I've observed that CEOs and entrepreneurs often don't appreciate other people telling them it's time to stop talking. So, I developed a forum meeting timer in a mobile app that allows members to keep track of their own time. **My Time**™ has an interactive timer and countdown clock that subconsciously motivates the speaker to stay on time. In addition to efficiently monitoring speaking time for individuals, **My Time** keeps forum meetings on schedule with clear visual aids for everyone in the room. To download My Time, scan the QR code below or visit the applicable website.

Apple:
http://itunes.apple.com/us/app/my-time-forum-meeting-timer/id522845145?mt=8

Android:
https://play.google.com/store/apps/details?id=com.kinetixx.MyTime

COACH

Sometimes in forum a member needs to share with the group an especially complex or sensitive issue, such as the sale of a business or a problem with a spouse. In these situations, another member acts as the presenter's coach or mentor. **The coach helps the presenter collect his or her thoughts and applicable information before the meeting and then guides the individual in how to best present the issue.** The coach also helps the member stay focused and on track during the presentation. The coach position is filled on a case-by-case basis by someone who has a genuine desire to mentor and help others.

TREASURER

The treasurer keeps the financial records for the forum. Members pay a nominal amount of money each year to conduct the business of the forum, such as rental fee for the meeting room, lunches, the retreat, etc. The treasurer tracks all income and expenses and pays any bills.

———————————

Just as a conductor cannot make music without the strings, woodwinds, brass and percussion, a facilitator cannot run the business of the forum without the process keeper, scribe, timekeeper, coach and treasurer. It takes everyone working together as a team to make the music of forum. Use the space on the following page to write down which members will fill each role in your forum.

MEMBER ROLES

Date: _____

Facilitator: _____

Assistant Facilitator: _____

Process Keeper: _____

Scribe: _____

Secondary Scribe: _____

Timekeeper: _____

Treasurer: _____

Coach (assigned as needed): _____

CHAPTER FOUR

THE PROCESS OF FOCUS FORUM

Now we will get into the nitty gritty of the Focus Forum process – specifically, how a forum meeting is run. I think of the steps of the forum process like traffic laws. We all break them at some point, in one way or another. We might exceed the speed limit or make an illegal U-turn. And while occasionally creeping through a stop sign might be okay, if you run stop signs on a regular basis, eventually you're going to crash, likely harming yourself and others.

The same is true in forum. **Deviating from the process here and there is fine; consistently ignoring it usually leads to trouble.** Sticking to the process is important because it keeps the forum in the "safe zone." As odd as it may seem, boundaries create freedom. The structure of the Focus Forum process creates a safe space for individual and group growth.

While it's important to follow the process, we must also account for the fact that human interaction is dynamic. **The most successful forums grow organically while adhering to the core steps. Focus Forum is about high performance and high return on the time invested by members, but each forum develops its own personality, norms and speed.**

In this chapter, I will explain the Focus Forum process step by step. Going through the process in detail puts every member "on the same page," with a clear understanding of what we do in a Focus Forum meeting, how we do it and why we do it that way. For each step, I will cover:

- What specifically to do during that segment of the meeting;

- How to do it based on best practices;

- Why we do it this way and what problems you will likely run into if you don't follow the process.

On the next page is an overview of the Focus Forum Process so that you can see it in its entirety from start to finish. This will give you context as we look at each of the steps.

FOCUS FORUM MEETING PROCESS

PRE-MEETING PREPARATION

- Update Sheet
- Prep work for Complex issues

FOCUS FORUM MEETING

- Alignment Exercise
- Updates
- Bio Break
- Assign Priorities
- Establish Presentation Order and Time Budget
- Presentations
  - Member Presents
  - Clarifying Questions
  - Feedback
  - Wrap-Up
- Housekeeping
- Closing Exercise

PRE-MEETING PREPARATION

WHAT: Update Sheet

Every member should complete an Update Sheet before every meeting. (You can copy the blank form in the Forms and Resources section or download it from **www.FocusForum.net**.) The Update Sheet provides a quick and easy way to capture what has happened in your business and life since the last meeting, what is happening now and what you likely will have to deal with before you see the group again.

HOW: The Focus Forum Update covers three key areas – business, family and personal – over three different time periods: past, current and future. The idea is to make brief notes about significant events, situations and challenges in each area of your life. (See the sample Update Sheet on the following page. Note that not every issue will have an entry in every time period.)

The business category covers anything that might be happening with your company, including issues with employees, partners, customers, lenders, sales, products, finances, acquisitions and legal concerns. Let's presume, for example, that you are dealing with an IRS audit. On your Update Sheet in the business section, you might write:

Past: *Got notice of IRS audit.*
Current: *Auditors are here now.*

Future: *How much money will I owe?*

The family category includes anything going on with your immediate or extended family, such as divorce or problems with a spouse, issues with children, health problems with parents, family dynamics involving siblings, etc. A family example might be:

Past: *Met with teachers re: Johnny's grades.*
Current: *May have learning disorder.*
Future: *Testing with specialist.*

The final category is personal. **Personal issues can include anything from health concerns to personal goals and accomplishments and anything in between.** People generally share rather freely about their businesses. They are less likely to share about their family and tend to have a difficult time sharing personal issues. But Focus Forum is about so much more than business. Forum is where we come to play our life's music, and that includes business, family and personal. So it's very important that you be willing to share your personal challenges as well as your family and business concerns.

The Update Sheet also quickly covers a few other areas, such as asking you to rate your current life situation and current health status on a scale of 1 to 10. It also includes a question regarding a topic you would like the group to study, which helps determine themes for the forum retreats.

FOCUS FORUM UPDATE SHEET

Date: _April 2, 2013_

(Keep in a folder. We will review these every year.)

This is a brief update about your life and the impact of events on you. List issues that you need feedback on or that will help others know you better. Focus on the best and worst of the past, present and future. Choose one topic that is most important at this time. **Be Specific. Be Brief.**

	PAST Things I'm dealing with from the past	PRESENT Things I'm dealing with now	FUTURE Things I will have to deal with before our next meeting
Business	1. Bully attorney 2. Contract collect 3. Lease true up	1. Pay me! 2. 3.	1. Selling South Hampton 2. Hire seasoned attorney 3. Management company problems
Family	1. Family to New Orleans 2. Grandkids ready for school 3.	1. Design show – sons 2. 3.	1. Estate planning 2. 3.
Personal	1. Skin getting old fast 2. 3.	1. Lose weight – sugar 2. Selling plane – emotions 3.	1. Newco forum business 2. 3.

List one topic that has been bugging you lately: _Responsible gun control_   On a scale of 1-10, how is your health? _8_

List one topic you would like the entire group to study: _Fun while aging_   On a scale of 1-10, how is your life? _8_

MUTUAL RESPECT GUIDELINES. Our forum is a family of caring people, giving and receiving advice on life's issues.

1) Attendance is expected at all meetings.
2) Being fully present (ready to give and receive) is mandatory.
3) Confidentiality is absolute.
4) Respect each other's time, feelings and fears. Be open and non-judgmental.
5) Speak only when it's your turn. No interruptions.

WHY: Completing the Update Sheet in advance focuses your thoughts and ideas and mentally prepares you for the forum meeting. It also helps you stay on task during the Update step. Pre-meeting preparation for forum is similar to the preparation you would do for a meeting with your attorney. You don't just walk in "cold turkey" – you give some thought in advance to what you want to cover. When the attorney is charging you by the minute, you want to get the most done in the shortest time. In Focus Forum, we cover more and get more value in the shortest possible time. To do that, everyone must come to the meeting prepared.

The Update Sheet is a snapshot in time that also serves as a reflection piece down the road. Each member should save all of their Update Sheets in a binder. At some point in the future – for example, at the retreat – you can pull out that binder and look back at your Updates. When viewed together, they show you what has happened in your life over the course of time. After a few years, you build a history that allows you to reflect on where you've been and determine if you are going in the right direction.

WHAT: Prep Work for Complex Issues

Occasionally a member will have a particularly complicated issue, such as the sale of a business, to present to the group. For these situations, detailed information should be prepared, sent and reviewed prior to the meeting.

HOW: Send in advance via email any handouts or information other members will need in order to provide feedback. (Of course, don't send anything that might jeopardize confidentiality or create a legal conflict.) If you are on the receiving end of this type of information, your commitment to the forum requires that you review the information prior to the meeting and be prepared to offer feedback. Remember the Golden Rule.

WHY: It is an inefficient use of members' time to try to explain all the nuances of a complex transaction during a meeting and then expect the group to come up with solutions on the spot. If a member wishes to get quality feedback on a complicated issue, they need to prepare the group in advance.

FOCUS FORUM MEETING

WHAT: Alignment Exercise

An opening exercise designed to focus everyone's attention on the forum.

HOW: The facilitator asks an interesting or thought-provoking question and then randomly allows each member to give a brief (one minute maximum) response.

WHY: When members arrive for a forum meeting, they are thinking about all kinds of other things – their businesses, their last phone call, problems at home, etc. Even once inside the room, they may be texting, checking email or talking in small groups. **The alignment exercise is a way to get everyone to switch gears and transition from outside mode into Focus Forum mode.**

The alignment exercise is similar to an orchestra tuning their instruments before a concert. When the conductor taps on the podium, that is the signal for the first violin to play the first note and for the musicians to tune their instruments to that one note. At the conclusion, all the instruments are in tune with one another, and the musicians are focused on the conductor, ready to play. Likewise, at the conclusion of the alignment exercise, everyone has their head in the room, ready to focus on the business of the forum. Without this, members likely will not be fully present and engaged in the meeting.

WHAT: Updates

Each member shares with the group the items from their Update Sheet. This is also the time to explain how we rate our current health and life situation (on the Update Sheet), briefly summarize the status of issues discussed at previous meetings, and give any additional information necessary to provide the group with an overall picture of our current situation.

HOW: The facilitator asks for **5 minutes of quiet time to allow members to review their Update Sheet or to quickly complete it if it wasn't done beforehand.** This time is to be used to prepare for your update, not to reconnect with other members. As you review your Update Sheet, eliminate topics you would discuss in a public setting (such as the purchase of a new car). Then, decide which issues you most want to get feedback and advice on.

Updates are an overview and only cover the crux of the issues; details are shared during the presentations later in the meeting. Updates generally take between 4 and 8 minutes per member and absolutely should not last longer than 10 minutes per person. **The facilitator gives his or her update first, followed by the other members in random order. The update is one directional, from the presenting member to the rest of the group.** So, there should be no questions, feedback or talking from other members.

During the updates, **the scribe captures the issues being mentioned by each person by writing them on a flipchart.** These notes should be simple and summary in nature yet include enough information so that members can recall 12 months later what they said. For example, if someone is talking about trying to get a loan at a bank, the scribe writes down "Bank loan." If another person shares that they are having problems with their partner, the scribe writes down "Partner." If the speaker repeats the same subject more than once, the scribe makes a check mark beside the word every time the person mentions it. This allows the person to know that they brought that issue up multiple times, and therefore it must be an important issue for them.

At the end of each update, the scribe asks the person speaking, "Did I capture?" Note that the scribe does not ask, "Did I capture what you said?" It is the presenter's responsibility to look at what was written down and either approve or change what was scribed. It is also the group's responsibility to review the scribed notes and indicate if something was left out or needs to be edited.

Occasionally during updates, members will ask for help with networking, for example, "Does anyone know how to get into XYZ company?" If another member indicates they can help with that, the facilitator asks them to connect "offline," meaning they should discuss it during break or outside the meeting since the subject does not involve the entire group.

WHY: The updates allow the forum to quickly get everyone's issues "on the table" so they can be prioritized. It is similar to a band or orchestra choosing the songs they will play and creating a set list. We have to find out which issues members need and want to talk about. Once we know what those are, we can prioritize them and create our forum "set list" – the issues we will discuss at this meeting.

WHAT: Bio Break

Bio breaks are for taking care of biological needs, ***not* for reconnecting with the office.**

HOW: The facilitator calls for the first bio break after the Updates and usually another bio break after half of the members have presented. However, any member may ask for a bio break at any time, and the meeting must stop to allow that person to go. Bio breaks are purposely kept short, typically between 4 and 7 minutes.

As you'll recall, one of the key norms that Focus Forum members commit to is being fully present. Being present is so important that most Focus Forums decide that members may not make phone calls, check email or voicemail or text during bio breaks. In those extremely rare situations when a member has a legitimate need to reconnect with the office, it should be brought up with the forum first.

WHY: The reason we do not allow members to reconnect during bio breaks is that it breaks the rhythm of the meeting, creates distractions and takes our attention and focus away from the forum, shortchanging not only our peers but ourselves as well. All it takes is just one person to reconnect with work to change the energy of the entire forum. One of the key characteristics of Focus Forum is that it addresses challenging issues yet moves quickly. **It is virtually impossible to be fully engaged in helping a peer address a difficult issue, disengage by checking email or dealing with a problem at the office during a bio break, and then step back into that space of being fully present again.**

WHAT: Assign Priorities

Members prioritize the issues they shared during Updates.

HOW: During the first bio break, each member goes to the flipchart where the scribe has captured their Update issues and prioritizes them by writing an "A" next to their most pressing issue and a "B" beside the next most pressing issue. (Because the forum is limited by time, only A and B priorities are assigned, even though there will be more issues scribed on the flipchart.)

WHY: Focus Forum is high performance, which means we cover more content in a shorter period of time than other types of forum. However, some groups decide to follow a more relaxed pace. Either way, a key element of Focus Forum is that **each person's time carries equal value**. Establishing priorities ensures that every member has the opportunity to present an issue and that each member's most critical issue is addressed.

Although every member usually has the chance to present an A priority, there is typically not enough time in the meeting for members to present their B priorities. So why, then, do we indicate B priorities at all? B priorities act like a compass – they give other forum members an understanding of which way our life is going and what other important issues we are dealing with.

WHAT: Establish Presentation Order and Time Budget

With the guidance of the facilitator, the group determines the order in which issues will be presented and establishes a time budget for the remainder of the meeting.

HOW: After members have assigned their A and B priorities and the group returns from the bio break, the facilitator asks who needs to present first. Once the group has established trust, members with emergency issues usually come forward readily. The facilitator assigns that issue as the first presentation and asks how much time the person will need to make their presentation. The facilitator then writes a "1" and the time allotment next to that issue on the flipchart.

Establishing the order for the rest of the presentations tends to happen organically. Someone in the group usually volunteers to go next. Seeing that other members' issues are more pressing, someone else might decide that their issue is not critical and volunteer to go last, or change their A priority to a B priority and elect not to present at all during this meeting. Once the first several presentations and the last presentation are determined, the other members typically self-assign their order. If not, the order is randomly assigned by the facilitator.

As the order of presentations is being established, the facilitator asks each member how long they need for their presentation and then writes the order number (1, 2, 3, 4, etc.) and the time allocation next to the applicable issue on the flipchart. When determining time allocations for each member's presentation, the facilitator adds 5 to 10 minutes for clarifying questions and 5 to 10 minutes for feedback to calculate a total time, and writes that total time next to the issue.

For example, a typical business issue usually takes 20 to 30 minutes total (10 minutes for the presentation, plus 5 to 10 minutes for questions and 5 to 10 minutes for feedback). Highly emotional topics such as divorce, major illness or placing a parent in a nursing home can take up to an hour. Over time, the forum establishes norms regarding how long certain types of presentations will take. At that point, creating the time budget becomes a quick and easy exercise.

Once time allocations have been set for all presentations, the facilitator adds up all the times (plus time for housekeeping and the closing exercise) to calculate the total time budget for the rest of the meeting. **Based on the time budget, the facilitator determines what time the meeting should end and gains agreement from every member to stay until the end.**

WHY: Establishing presentation order and developing a time budget is crucial for a number of reasons. First, it ensures that the most critical issues are addressed up front and that there is enough time for all members to present. Second, it creates the timeline that keeps the meeting on track and determines the total duration of the meeting. And finally, it lets members know how much time they have to present. Without a time budget, people tend to ramble when they give a presentation or provide feedback. The time budget provides the framework for the timekeeper to give time checks or for members using the My Time mobile app to self-correct.

PRESENTATIONS

Following the order previously established by the group, **members present their issues to the forum. The group's job is to analyze the information presented, ask clarifying questions and then offer feedback and advice based on their life and business experiences.** Throughout the presentation portion of the meeting, the facilitator and process keeper monitor the process, and the timekeeper monitors the time in relation to the time budget. Because entrepreneurs and CEOs generally don't appreciate others telling them what to do (i.e., a timekeeper telling them to stop talking), I recommend each member use the My Time™ mobile app mentioned earlier to keep time for their presentation.

From a time perspective, presentations comprise the largest part of a forum meeting. This is when the real "work" of forum is done. Likewise, from a value perspective, this is often when members get the most benefit from their forum experience. It's important to remember, however, that **what you get out of forum is directly related to what you put into it.**

Focus Forum is mental exercise – it's the equivalent of going to the gym for a physical workout, but for your brain. To get any benefit from going to the gym, you have to do the work. Now most people at the gym are serious about improving themselves. They are the ones sweating, giving it their all, not worried about how they look or what others think of them. But some people – I call them "posers" – are there more to be seen than to work out.

The same is true in forum. Those who are willing to put in the effort and to give it their all – speak their truth, be vulnerable, share their emotions – will reap the rewards. The posers in a forum are those who won't fully put their issues on the table for fear of what others might think of them or who must make sure they look like the smartest people in the room. Posers neither get much value out of forum nor give much back to the group. In forum, just like at the gym, you can simply hang out or you can be serious about working out and improving yourself. The choice is yours.

WHAT: Member Presents

Each member presents their A priority issue, no matter whether it is a business, family or personal problem. In my years in forum, I have heard just about every kind of issue, challenge and problem imaginable. On the business side, people have shared about legal troubles, employee problems and partners who embezzled from them. I've heard many entrepreneurs talk about how their best friend/business partner is not pulling their weight or wants their child to come to work in the business. With respect to family issues, people have shared everything from, "I'm not sure my wife loves me anymore" to "My adult son won't speak to me" or "I think my dad has early Alzheimer's, and I'm the one who has to deal with it."

Over time as the forum develops trust, people become more open with their personal challenges. I've been in forums where people talked about finding out they had cancer or their spouse was having an affair. Some have admitted to affairs themselves. When given the opportunity in a safe environment, it is surprising how many people want to talk about their problems and get them off their chest.

HOW: The member lays out the issue in as concise a manner as possible, generally describing the nature of the problem, what they have done about it and how they feel about it. For complex business issues, the presenter should send briefing material prior to the meeting for members to review in advance. Presentations last from 10 minutes for a typical business issue to 30 minutes for a highly emotional family or personal issue.

During the member's presentation, no one is to ask questions. This one-way flow of information allows the presenter to stay focused. **Other forum members are actively listening** not only to what is being said, but also to what is being communicated (that is, what is *not* being said). The scribe does not take notes during presentations. However, members can make notes about clarifying questions they might like to ask. Some people cannot actively listen and take notes at the same time; others find that they actually listen better when taking notes. Do what works best for you to help you stay actively engaged.

WHY: Men in particular have few places where they can talk openly and share their thoughts. Focus Forum is a safe place where they can let down their guard and share their emotions. What makes Focus Forum a safe environment is that every member commits to follow the shared value norms and the process norms. Trust is built upon confidentiality and a shared life. During the presentations is when all of that comes to bear. If people are to fully and openly share their life's challenges, the commitment to confidentiality, mutual respect, honesty and being fully present must be upheld.

WHAT: Clarifying Questions

After the presentation, the other members ask clarifying questions. **I tend to think of this part of the meeting as a game of smart people trying to ask the right questions in the right way to help the presenter find the answer on their own.**

HOW: Clarifying questions typically take 5 to 10 minutes. Their purpose is twofold. The more obvious purpose is to help the listener better understand the issue, for example, "What did you mean when you said…?" The second, more important purpose is to **help the presenter think through the problem on their own.** If the presenter is having trouble getting a bank loan, for instance, members might ask "smart" questions such as:

> *"Have you completed the financial ratio analysis the bank is looking for?"*
>
> *"Who do you know that knows the loan officer?"*
>
> *"What personality type is the loan officer?"*

"What do you personally have in common with the loan officer?"

WHY: A great quote by Benjamin Franklin states, **"Tell me and I forget, teach me and I may remember, involve me and I learn."** When people are skillfully led to draw their own conclusions or find their own answers, they are more likely to learn from the experience. Presenters are more likely to implement solutions they help craft rather than solutions they are given by other forum members.

WHAT: Feedback

Offering constructive feedback and advice is the primary way members give back to the forum. This is how we share our expertise and wisdom to help one another. Focus Forum is a two-way street – we receive great benefit from the experience, but we must also give something of value. We do that by carefully listening to presenters and then offering the best advice possible. **We may not think our opinion will be of any real value, but we never know when it may be the one little tidbit that helps a presenter better understand their problem.**

HOW: The facilitator goes around the table, usually sequentially, asking each member to give feedback. Responses are limited to two minutes per person. To solicit appropriate feedback, the facilitator frames questions for the group in three categories: *see, hear, feel*. For example:

> *"What problems do you see that this person needs to solve?"*
>
> *"What did you hear this person say or communicate?"*
>
> *"What do you feel this person needs based on your personal experience?"*

The facilitator might also frame the feedback with questions such as, "If this was you, how would you handle it?" or "In your experience, what did you do when this kind of thing happened?"

I am a strong proponent of every member giving the presenter feedback. I think it is a bit like cheating for a member to simply agree with or to "second" something another member has said. At a minimum, members need to give a specific reason why they agree with advice that has already been given. (If a member says they don't have any feedback to give, most often it is because they were not fully listening to the presentation.)

When giving feedback, members should use clean talk and forum speak. As you may recall from earlier in the book, clean talk is telling the truth – in all respects. Forum is not about telling people what you think they want to hear. Nor is it about embellishing your own experiences. You are there to get and give advice, not to win a popularity contest.

Forum speak means speaking from your personal experience rather than "shoulding" on the presenter (i.e., "You *should* do…" or "You *should have* done…"). If you have direct personal experience with a similar situation, you would start your feedback with, "When a similar situation happened to me, this is how I handled it…." Be sure to share what you did right, as well as any mistakes you might have made or ways you could have handled the situation better. If you don't have direct experience with a situation, you can start your feedback with, "I don't have personal experience with something like this, but if it were me, here is how I think I would deal with it…."

WHY: The facilitator frames the feedback with specific questions to guide members in giving the presenter the type of feedback and advice he/she needs. When members give their feedback sequentially, each person tends to build on the previous feedback and focus on how they can make the feedback better. The result is very high-quality feedback for the presenter.

WHAT: Wrap-Up

The facilitator brings closure to each presentation by trying to gauge how the presenter is feeling.

HOW: The facilitator asks the presenter a question such as, "Did you get what you needed?" or "Do you have finishing comments?" or "Was this helpful?"

I have found that simply saying, "Yes, thank you" is often the best response to feedback. We tend to have a need to respond in some way to feedback, and yet we often need time to absorb and process what has been shared with us. **Saying "Thank you" fills that uncomfortable space while recognizing the gift of feedback that we have just received.**

Of course, there are times when the presenter truly needs additional feedback from the group. If that is the case, the facilitator asks the group if it's okay to spend a few more minutes on the topic, being mindful of the overall time budget. Or, members with specific expertise that could be helpful to the presenter can discuss the issue one-on-one with him/her after the meeting.

WHY: Presentation closure is important for two reasons. First, it serves as the transition from one presenter and his/her issue to the next presenter. More importantly, it gives the group a sense of where the presenter's head is at and if the presenter has the information necessary to move forward and address the issue.

WHAT: Housekeeping

This is the opportunity for the group to quickly address any logistical issues related to the forum, such as scheduling future meetings, planning the retreat or discussing financial issues.

HOW: The facilitator addresses any pertinent issues and confirms the date and time for the next meeting. **It's best to schedule all meetings for the year at one time and then adjust as needed.** If a member has a conflict with a scheduled meeting, it is up to that person to lead the discussion to reschedule the meeting for a time when all can attend. (We call this The Rule of the Problem – **if you create a problem, you must solve the problem.**)

For financial issues, the person who handles the money for the forum gives a quick update on any forum expenses, such as food and drink, or rental fee for the meeting space.

WHY: The Housekeeping segment sets aside a few dedicated moments each meeting to address the necessary business and logistical issues of the forum. **Covering housekeeping issues at the end of the meeting encourages the group to reach consensus faster.**

WHAT: Closing Exercise

A quick, simple exercise designed to bring closure to the meeting and to gauge how members are thinking and feeling.

HOW: The facilitator asks a simple question such as, "In less than 30 seconds, what did you learn today?" or

"Give me one word that describes what you are feeling right now."

WHY: The closing exercise is very important as it **gives everyone, especially the facilitator, an indication of how each member is doing mentally and emotionally.** If everyone around the table except for one person says the meeting was great or enlightening, we know something is going on with one person. This also cues the facilitator or a close friend to talk more with the person after the meeting.

While at first glance the Focus Forum meeting process may seem involved, once you've gone through the process a few times, you will see how straightforward and powerful the process actually is. On the following page is a summary to use during forum meetings that will quickly guide you through the process until, after several meetings, the process becomes second nature.

Focus Forum is specifically designed to provide greater value and benefit for members by accomplishing more in less time, and the process is the key to accomplishing that. To underscore the importance of the process to forum success, let's revisit our orchestra analogy. When every musician plays the same notes in the same key at the same tempo, the result is beautiful music. But if one musician plays in another key or off tempo, it negatively affects not only the other musicians, but the music itself. It is the rigid structure imposed by specific notes, keys and tempos that allows a group of musicians to produce music far grander than what any one musician could produce by himself.

The same is true in Focus Forum. When a member doesn't follow the process – for example by not being fully present, reconnecting with the office during a meeting, should-ing on a presenter during feedback or not having mutual commitment and respect with the rest of the group – it negatively affects the other members as well as the culture of the forum. It is the structure provided by shared norms and the Focus Forum process that creates the framework that allows the group to grow organically and create something more powerful than the individual members.

FOCUS FORUM MEETING SUMMARY

TIME	EVENT	NOTES
15-30 min	Pre-Meeting Prep	Complete Forum Update Sheet (download from **www.FocusForum.net**) and review advance information
1 min/member max; 10 min total	Alignment Exercise	Transition to forum mode
5 min group review; 4-8 min/update	Updates	Quiet review of Update Sheet, then each member shares from Update Sheet
4-7 min	Bio Break	NO reconnecting with office
During bio break	Assign Priorities	Write "A" next to most pressing issue and "B" beside the next most pressing issue
5 min	Establish Presentation Order & Time Budget	Emergencies followed by "A" priorities
PRESENTATIONS		
10-30 min/ member	Member Presents	Each member presents "A" priority issue
5-10 min total	Clarifying Questions	Members ask "smart" questions
2 min/member max; 15 min total	Feedback	Members offer constructive feedback using forum speak and clean talk
5 min	Wrap-up	Concludes and brings closure to presentation
10-15 min	Housekeeping	Business issues of forum
5 min	Closing Exercise	Check in with each member

CHAPTER FIVE

THE FOCUS FORUM RETREAT

Retreats are an integral part of Focus Forum. They offer rare opportunities to get away from the busyness of life and the distractions of running a business to focus on development and growth. Forum retreats serve many purposes. They provide both the opportunity and the environment to:

- Allow members to explore their thoughts and opinions about themselves and others in their life.

- Use the forum as a tool to help members become better all-around people;

- Re-evaluate the forum as a whole and reflect on how each member fits and functions within the group;

- Introduce a new member into the group;

- Review the norms, confidentiality and each member's commitment to the forum;

● Evaluate what went well the past year and what
can be improved upon for the coming year.

One retreat per year is essential for every forum.
Some mature forums have two retreats per year with the
second one focused on a common hobby, such as hunting.
Retreats are typically a minimum of two days, with three
days being the optimum. Like other types of retreats, a
forum retreat should be held at an offsite location, far
enough away so that members cannot go home at night
and reconnect. The location can be anything from a
resort to a member's mountain or beach house, and it
should have a meeting place large enough for the group
to congregate.

Focus Forum retreats are part "work" and part "play."
Mornings are typically spent on individual and group
exercises (the "work"), while afternoons are spent doing
leisure activities as a group (the "play"). Some "work"
exercises are fairly basic and revolve around subjects that
generally don't have a high emotional charge, such as
discussions about personal values, health, and business
issues like key employees. A great basic retreat exercise
is to have each member complete a personality profile
such as the Myers-Briggs or DiSC and then share their
results with the group.

By design, other exercises are more personal, often more
emotionally charged and involve deeper introspection.

One exercise typically conducted at every retreat is a "personal review," in which each member reviews their scribed sheets from the year's meetings and does a self-directed examination of their life for the past year. Another deeper exercise is what we call a "lifeline exercise," where each member talks about their life in five-year increments from the time they were born to the time they expect to die.

Afternoon leisure activities offer members the chance to talk with each other, share life stories and get to know one another better. Examples include golf, hiking, skeet shooting, beach football, boating or rafting, or skydiving.

Each retreat has a theme. Several months prior to the retreat, the group has a discussion at a forum meeting regarding trends from the answers to the questions on the Update Sheet, "What has been bugging you lately?" and "What topic would you like the entire group to study?" These trends help determine the theme for the retreat. Here are some examples of retreat themes I've used in the past: *Giving Back. Lessons My Father Taught Me. 10-Year Goals.*

Logistically, retreats are fairly straightforward. The facilitator-elect of the forum is in charge of planning the retreat. He/she assigns members of the forum responsibilities for various tasks, such as finding the location, arranging transportation, developing the program and coordinating the food. At the retreat itself, all members pitch in to help with daily responsibilities and duties.

Retreats can get very expensive, and the budget should be made keeping in mind the member who least can afford it. It is imperative that every forum member attend the retreat, and we don't want to put an unreasonable financial burden on anyone. If there is money in the treasury, that can be used to reduce the cost for everyone. If the retreat is held at a member's home, the budget should include money for cleaning and any other incidentals.

Retreats are the foundation of a fully functioning forum. They are life-changing experiences in which members can make powerful new discoveries about themselves and their forum peers.

CONCLUSION

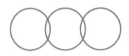

My forum experiences have been some of the most
rewarding – as well as some of the most frustrating –
times of my life. The best experiences were when the
chemistry of the group worked, and a great deal of the
chemistry within a forum is based upon having similar
values about how to treat each other.

When forums didn't work as well, it was often because
the forum's culture was not developed or not strong
enough to openly and honestly have meaningful dialogue
and accept each other's unique differences. Other times,
it was because some members' egos and needs
overshadowed the forum.

I wrote this book as a guide to help you maximize the
benefits and minimize the risks of forum. The strength
of this book is that it creates rules of conduct. These
rules are not set in stone, but rather guidelines to create
a safe environment that allow for a high quality and

high volume of experiences. The more the group deviates from the Focus Forum process, the greater the risks.

But be forewarned – **interaction between humans at any level carries with it great risk of misunderstanding.** Even if you follow the process to the letter, there will always be a risk of conflict. Such is the nature of human interactions, especially among high-performance individuals.

I wish you luck with your forum, and I welcome your questions, as well as your feedback about what works and what doesn't, at wmasters@kinetixx.com.

Focus Forum is an ever-evolving journey of learning. It is a place to make life's music together – to gain a deeper understanding of ourselves and our lives through connections with others and their life experiences. The process of forum is the foundation that allows that to happen. When we play out of turn or out of sync, we lose harmony within the group. But when everyone plays their music to the same beat, the results are incredible; and our lives are ever richer for the experience.

Bill

FOCUS FORUM FAQS

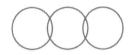

MEMBERSHIP

Q: *What is the optimum number of members for a forum?*

A: Focus Forum intentionally limits membership to six to eight members so that every member gets "air time." Six is the minimum to ensure good feedback, and eight tends to be the maximum to allow everyone to present and still keep the meeting within four to five hours.

Q: *How long does a forum stay together?*

A: Theoretically indefinitely, because as people leave, new members are brought in to keep the forum going. It's rare that a forum completely disbands, but it does happen. Just like some relationships, some forums never develop the "chemistry" necessary to sustain the group long term. Good forums that work last a lifetime. As members retire from their main professions, the forum still meets but tends to have fewer meetings per year. Some of these mature forums morph into couples' forums. When a forum has been together a very long time, members often pursue a specific activity that most, if not all, members enjoy, particularly during retreats. Examples include hunting, fishing, golf, skeet shooting, whitewater and self-improvement activities.

Q: *What happens if a member leaves the group?*

A: I have found that one universal weakness of forums that are predominantly male is that the need of high-performance men to have a place to vent is so strong that most will tolerate a very bad forum over leaving a forum. That said, it is fairly common for members to leave a forum, and it happens for a number of different reasons. Sometimes, people just lose interest, or their lives are so busy that they can't commit the time to forum. In these situations, the facilitator should talk to the person and try to determine what is going on. Oftentimes, a member takes a job in a different city and moves away. In that case, it is the member's choice as to whether he or she will make the trip to come back for forum meetings.

Some people simply aren't the right fit with the group. If you feel that you are not a good fit with your group, I encourage you to leave and find another forum that is a better fit for you. However, unless there is a major conflict of interest, I strongly recommend you stay with the forum for one year, because it takes time to build the relationships and culture that make a forum successful.

Q: *How do you remove someone from a forum?*

A: Removing a forum member is somewhat analogous to a divorce in a marriage. Consequently, it is very difficult and should be dealt with carefully and gently. Ideally, members should self-remove (discussed in the next question) rather than putting the forum in the difficult position of having to ask them to leave. However, before a situation reaches the point of removal, the facilitator should discuss with the person the behaviors or actions that are causing a problem, as well as suggestions to correct the problem. Then the member should be given time to resolve the problem. If the problem persists and the member does not self-remove, the removal of that member must be handled openly and procedurally. Otherwise, the rest of the forum members will never fully trust that they won't be asked to leave also.

Q: *What is self-removal?*

A: One of the key principles of forum is this: **If you bring a problem or conflict to the forum, then you need to solve the problem or get out.** If something you've done will harm the rest and cannot be resolved, you should voluntarily leave the forum rather than forcing the forum to ask you to leave. Self-removal can result from nonparticipation, a confidentiality breach, an unresolved conflict or a major personality difference with another member.

Q: *How does a forum bring in a new member?*

A: It's crucial that new members be a good fit with the forum's culture. Consequently, potential members should be vetted through a rigorous process:

● The "sponsoring" member interviews the candidate to determine if they are a fit with the group.

● The entire group discusses the candidate, and if the forum is interested, every member interviews the candidate.

● The group conducts a blind vote on whether to invite the candidate to join the forum. (A blind vote is a "yes" or "no" written on a piece of paper, put in a box and counted by the facilitator.) A new member is invited to join only with a 100 percent blind vote of the entire forum. **If there is just one "no" vote, the person is not invited into the forum.** No discussion, no questions asked.

● If the candidate is unanimously voted in, they are invited to a forum meeting after which they decide if they will commit to the forum for at least one year.

● If the candidate commits, it is best to officially bring them into the group during the retreat (if it is to be held within a few months).

Q: *What happens if a forum would like to bring in a member of the opposite gender, such as a male forum bringing in a female or a female forum bringing in a male?*

A: In my experience, if a forum wants to bring in someone of the opposite gender, there needs to be at least two people of the other gender. This makes everyone more comfortable and also helps all members' spouses to be less suspicious.

Q: *Should best friends or family members (such as a brother or brother-in-law) be in the same forum?*

A: Absolutely not. This weakens relationships, both inside and outside the forum. No one should ever be put in the situation of having to choose between the forum and family/friends.

TIME

Q: *How often does a forum meet?*

A: Forums generally meet a minimum of eight times per year plus a retreat. Many forums take a month off during the summer because of vacations and, rather than have a meeting during the holidays, will have a Christmas dinner with spouses.

Q: *How long does a forum meeting last?*

A: The length of a typical forum meeting can be estimated at 40 minutes per member. This generally gives enough time for each member to present at least one subject. With six members, that equates to about four hours; with eight members, about five and a half hours. A very efficient forum might average 30 minutes per member, but this requires extreme discipline and absolutely no outside distractions.

Attendance

Q: *What happens if members miss meetings?*

A: **Forum attendance is mandatory.** Each forum develops their own norms regarding how to handle absences. Typically, one absence per year for a legitimate reason is excused; however, the member must explain to the group why he or she missed the meeting. The second absence is unexcused, and any additional absences require self-removal unless the absences are approved by a 100 percent blind vote of the forum.

Q: *What happens if members are late to meetings?*

A: In Focus Forum, **everyone's time is equal.** Members who arrive late to meetings take away from other members' time. In some forums, arriving late is either excused or non-excused, as decided by the group on a case-by-case basis. Other forums create norms such as being late two times equals one absence. Another typical norm is that the member must pay $10 per every late minute into the treasury of the forum. (If the person makes a joke and does not pay into the forum, that is considered a major violation of forum protocol. **No member can excuse themselves from forum norms.**) Either of these approaches should solve the problem quickly.

Q: *What happens if members leave meetings early?*

A: It depends on each forum's norms. Some forums have a rule that if a member leaves early three times per year, for any reason, it equals one unexcused missed meeting. (And if a certain number of missed meetings requires self-removal, this tends to solve the leaving-early problem.) In other forums, leaving early can be either excused or non-excused. To be excused, an early departure must be for a critical reason as agreed upon by the group. If the member leaves early for a non-critical reason, such as a social event, the group needs to discuss and consider whether that member is committed to the forum.

CONFLICTS

Q: *What happens if someone creates a problem for the forum?*

A: A key principle of forum is **"clean up your own mess."** If a member creates a problem or conflict for the forum, they are fully responsible for solving the problem with the least amount of time and damage to anyone in the forum. If the member can't solve the problem, they should immediately self-remove.

Q: *What happens if someone breaches the forum's confidentiality?*

A: Since **confidentiality is the backbone of forum, any and all breaches are serious and must be dealt with.** There are two kinds of confidentiality breach: intentional and unintentional. If it is clear that a breach was intentional, then the member removes himself. If the member does not self-remove, the forum has no choice but to remove the person because there is seldom any chance of reconciliation in the case of an intentional confidentiality breach.

Unintentional confidentiality breaches are usually honest mistakes and can vary from minor to critical. If the person who commits the breach does not want to stay in the forum, they can self-remove and quickly solve the problem. If the person does want to stay in the forum, how the situation is handled depends on the forum.

In some forums, the member who committed the unintentional breach must come forward and give a presentation to the group explaining how and why the breach happened. (This would take the place of their regular presentation at a meeting.) The facilitator may choose to create a small committee to hear the breach before it is presented to the full forum. At some point, however, the entire forum has to address the breach and come to a resolution. Often, if the breach is minor, the forum will allow the member to stay.

Otherwise, the member is asked to leave the forum.

Other forums have norms that any confidentiality breach – even an unintentional, minor breach – requires immediate self-removal. The forum then has the opportunity to discuss the breach and choose whether they want to invite the member back. If the member is invited back and accepts, the breach has to be addressed and the confidentiality issue discussed.

Q: *How does a forum handle confidential business information?*

A: If public companies are involved, Sarbanes-Oxley rules apply. Mergers and acquisitions and trade secrets also present confidentiality issues. All of these should be treated with caution within a forum as there are risks associated with them.

Q: *Can members be deposed for things said in a forum?*

A: Most likely, so it's best to stay away from topics that might create that situation or possibly bring in the applicable member's lawyer to advise.

Q: *How should a forum handle conflicts of interest?*

A: If a member decides to go into business with another member, one of them must leave the forum, because having business partners in the same forum creates significant conflict. In addition, if a member would like to go into a business that conflicts with an existing member's business (usually defined as a direct competitor to their core business), then the one creating the problem for the forum needs to self-remove.

Q: *How should a forum handle personality conflicts?*

A: If personality conflicts arise among members, those involved must solve it themselves and not bring it into the forum. The rest of the forum must stay neutral and stay out of the conflict in order to prevent a division within the group. If they can't resolve the conflict, all of those involved should self-remove, so as to not force one person or another into leaving. In addition, if only one were to leave or be forced out, the other forum members would likely always have in the back of their minds (but never voice it) that they must not cross the member who stayed. Knowing that all will have to self-remove motivates people to work out their differences.

Q: *How do you handle a clique within the forum?*

A: Inclusiveness is at the heart of forum. Cliques separate the forum into smaller groups, break the forum bonds and can create both real and imagined exclusions. Consequently, cliques should be avoided at all times. If a member feels excluded, he/she should first discuss the matter in private with the facilitator who will then bring the issue to the group. Of course, it is common for likeminded people (such as those who like to hunt, fish, golf or enjoy certain sports) to gravitate toward each other in a forum. This is natural and okay, as long as they keep conversations about their common interest outside of the forum.

Q: *Can forum members do business together?*
A: Absolutely not. If two members want to do business together, at least one needs to self-remove and preferably both need to leave. When members start doing business together, it changes the entire dynamic of the forum.

Q: *Can forum members buy and sell goods to each other?*
Forum members can buy and sell goods to each other personally, such as a car or boat, but it should always be offered at the "friends and family" price. Buying and selling items of substantial value should be highly avoided. All transactions between forum members should be evaluated on the basis of whether they could easily lead to conflict and if those risks are acceptable to the group.

Q: *Can forum members invest together?*
A: Members absolutely cannot invest in each other's businesses. Members may join together to invest in a business that is not in the forum or in another investment opportunity, but there must be full disclosure to the forum.

Q: *Can a member ask another member for an investment?*

A: **Absolutely not.** Under no circumstances should any forum member request an investment from another member, as that will always create conflict.

MEMBER ISSUES

Q: *What happens when a member sells a business or is in the process of selling a business?*

A: The sale of a business is a major life event and an exceptional opportunity to "walk life" with the member. During the sale, the forum should actively support the member and be involved in any way the member requests.

Q: *What if someone within a forum has to declare bankruptcy?*

A: Bankruptcy is no different than any other problem that might be brought up in a forum. Every effort should be made to help the member, either offering feedback from personal or indirect experiences or suggesting resources.

Q: *What if someone in the forum appears to have depression?*

A: Depression is common among a large portion of the population. If forum members believe another member is suffering from depression, it should be addressed privately with the facilitator. The person may need medical attention, and if they choose not to seek medical attention, then it would be incumbent upon the forum to compassionately suggest (not demand) that the person seek medical attention.

MISCELLANEOUS

Q: *Is alcohol allowed at meetings?*

A: **Alcohol is never allowed during meetings.** After a meeting and during social activities, alcohol is certainly permitted. During the retreat, alcohol is not permitted during any of the formal exercises. A shared drink is fine after the hard work of forum or a conflict has been dealt with. If an issue should arise after alcohol is introduced, it must be forum norm that the issue is tabled and discussed later – *no exceptions.*

Q: *What happens to the scribed notes from meetings?*

A: **Scribed notes are captured but not distributed because they are highly confidential.** The notes are brought to the retreat and become the backbone of a key retreat exercise. The assistant facilitator keeps the notes, as he/she will be responsible for the retreat.

OTHER TYPES OF FORUMS

Q: *Can forum be used within an organization?*

A: Yes. In fact, forums within organizations break down barriers and help people work together more effectively. I know of a hospital that uses forum protocol within functional groups. In an organization, the forum will be more focused toward the needs of the organization and less focused on the needs of the individual.

Q: *Can a forum be used with common interest groups?*

A: Absolutely. Forum works because it allows people to share life experiences. The forum process can be used by groups of people with common life situations, such as a certain disease (like cancer) and even pregnant women.

FORMS
AND
RESOURCES

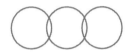

Focus Forum Update Sheet

Date: _____
(Keep in a folder. We will review these every year.)

This is a brief update about your life and the impact of events on you. List issues that you need feedback on or that will help others know you better. Focus on the best and worst of the past, present and future. Choose one topic that is most important at this time. **Be Specific. Be Brief.**

	PAST Things I'm dealing with from the past	**PRESENT** Things I'm dealing with now	**FUTURE** Things I will have to deal with before our next meeting
Business	1. _____ 2. _____ 3. _____	1. _____ 2. _____ 3. _____	1. _____ 2. _____ 3. _____
Family	1. _____ 2. _____ 3. _____	1. _____ 2. _____ 3. _____	1. _____ 2. _____ 3. _____
Personal	1. _____ 2. _____ 3. _____	1. _____ 2. _____ 3. _____	1. _____ 2. _____ 3. _____

List one topic that has been bugging you lately: _____
On a scale of 1-10, how is your health? _____

List one topic you would like the entire group to study: _____
On a scale of 1-10, how is your life? _____

MUTUAL RESPECT GUIDELINES. Our forum is a family of caring people, giving and receiving advice on life's issues.

1) Attendance is expected at all meetings.
2) Being fully present (ready to give and receive) is mandatory.
3) Confidentiality is absolute.
4) Respect each other's time, feelings and fears. Be open and non-judgmental.
5) Speak only when it's your turn. No interruptions.

SAMPLE FOCUS FORUM NORMS CONSTITUTION

Focus Forum is a group of dedicated individuals who agree to come together at planned intervals to share life experiences in order for each to grow in body, mind and spirit.

We commit to each other the following:

1. Confidentiality always and forever
   a. Any breach or perceived breach of confidentiality is brought to the attention of the facilitator immediately and confidentially.
   b. Any breach brought to the facilitator is addressed with the parties involved within one week.
   c. Any breach is presented to the forum at the next meeting, whether or not it was resolved between the parties.
   d. If the breach is clear cut, the member who breached confidentiality will resign. Should the member ask to be reinstated, the forum can decide to allow the member back only by blind vote of 100 percent of the remaining members.
   e. All breaches – minor or major – are openly discussed by the group as a learning experience.

2. Mutual respect
   a. Abide by The Golden Rule – we treat each other as we would like to be treated.

    b. We put ourselves in the other person's shoes and see from their perspective.

    c. There is absolutely no outside communication during any presentation.

    d. We speak first from our personal experience.

3. Mutual commitment

    a. Each member's time carries equal value.

    b. We actively listen to one another's updates and presentations.

    c. We are engaged in the process as if we are players in a championship sports game.

4. Honesty

    a. We acknowledge that honesty requires the willingness and openness to both give and receive the truth.

    b. We shine light on our own shadows before offering advice to others.

5. Active participation

    a. We are fully present, "in the game," and treat every point as if it is a match point.

    b. We are open to both give and receive.

    c. We practice mindfulness.

6. Pledge to keep the process

    a. We attend every meeting with no more than two absences.

b. We are on time, every time and stay the full time. We agree to pay a $10 per minute fee if late.

c. We focus on fast, accurate communication.

d. The retreat is mandatory attendance.

We individually and collectively commit to these norms for the 12 months or until our next retreat.

Date: _____

Facilitator: _____

Assist. Facilitator: _____

Scribe: _____

Assist. Scribe: _____

Members:_____

_____

_____

_____

_____

_____

RECOMMENDED READING

A Goal is a Dream with a Deadline: Extraordinary Wisdom for Entrepreneurs, Managers, and Other Smart People, by Leo Helzel (McGraw-Hill Trade, 1995)

If... (Questions for the Game of Life), by Evelyn McFarlane and James Saywell (Villard, 1995)

Please Understand Me: Character and Temperament Types, by David Keirsey and Marilyn Bates (B & D Books, 1984)

Power Questions: Build Relationships, Win New Business, and Influence Others, by Andrew Sobel and Jerold Panas (Wiley, 2012)

Snakes in Suits: When Psychopaths Go to Work, by Paul Babiak and Robert D. Hare (HarperBusiness, 2007)

NOTES

NOTES

NOTES

NOTES

Acknowledgements

I wish to express a heartfelt thank you to the members of all the forums I have been involved with, whether as a member, a moderator/facilitator or an advisor/coach. The journeys of discovery, the retreats, the highs and the lows, the understandings and the misunderstandings – each of these influenced my life and this book.

I would like to extend a special thank you to the passionate, dedicated members of the YPO International Forum Advisory Board, with whom I served from 1994 to 2000 and who saw me through both good times and bad, and especially the sale of my business.

I am also deeply grateful to those entrepreneurs whom I instructed on how to start a forum as well as the process of Focus Forum. Their inner gratification and dedication to their forums has been my reward. I am certain that their business will be the stars of job creation in the future through better understanding.

I wish to thank my family for their love and untold patience in regards to my frequent discourse about how people can become their best and my incessant exploration of how to create systems that foster communication among high-performance people.

I am also deeply grateful to Juli Baldwin, without whom this book would not have been completed, for her persistence, expert advice and resources in making this book possible.

ABOUT THE AUTHOR

Bill Masters is an extremely successful entrepreneur whose accomplishments span more than 30 years of inventing, building, designing, manufacturing and developing consumer products. Bill has started numerous  companies, including international businesses in England and New Zealand. He founded Perception Kayaks (a kayak-building company) in 1976, grew the business to the largest of its kind in the world and then successfully sold it. He holds over 30 patents in boat design, plastics manufacturing, computers and heat transfer, including landmark patents in 3-D printing. He is currently president and owner/partner in several companies.

Bill has always had a passion for developing and mentoring high-performance entrepreneurs. He has served that purpose by dedicating his time to studying and advancing the art and science of forum. Bill played an active role on the International Forum Advisory Boards for both Young Presidents' Organization (YPO) and World Presidents' Organization (WPO), and at one point, as a forum officer, was responsible for all YPO forums in North America.

Bill also shares his time and experience with numerous organizations, committees and boards. He sat on the boards of Clemson University and Furman University, served as Chairman of the Charlotte, N.C. Federal Reserve Bank Board and was chosen as a delegate to the White House Conference on Small Business. He was also selected to be Mayor of the Whitewater Village for the 1996 Summer Olympics.

Bill earned his B.S. Degree in Engineering from Clemson University. He has received numerous accolades and awards throughout his career, including Entrepreneur of the Year from the Society of International Business Fellows, Entrepreneur of the Year for the State of South Carolina from *Inc. Magazine* and Person of the Year for South Carolina from the Small Business Administration.

Bill is married to Dr. Anne Graham Masters, MD. He has two sons, Nathan and Adam (both boot-strap entrepreneurs), and one daughter, Allyson. He currently resides with his family in Greenville, S.C. You can contact Bill at wmasters@kinetixx.com.

Made in the USA
Columbia, SC
20 February 2022

56510771R00061